FOLLOW UP
SAVVY

BY WANDA ALLEN

ISBN 0983909903

ISBN 9780983909903

Author: Wanda Allen, followupsavvy.com

Cover Design / Graphics: Jennifer Swan Myers, Swan Design www.swandesignonline.com

Editor: Adrienne Moch, www.adriennemoch.com

Layout Design: Cheryl Perez, www.yourepublished.com

To order this book, go to followupsavvy.com

ACKNOWLEDGMENTS

To my family: my parents, Tony and Roberta, and my sisters, Rhonda and Jacque. You've been my constant support system. I thank you for understanding my need to make a career change and walking away from 25 years of banking. I knew there was a new life waiting for me; your love and support gave me the confidence to explore and discover what it was. I've been able to pursue the journey I'm on and my life is forever changed. You're the best family anyone could ask for. I'm blessed to have all of you in my life.

To Ritchie, my husband: Thank you for being my #1 fan. You provided amazing support during my career change as well. I know it was a scary move. In spite of your feelings, you gave me nothing but words of encouragement to keep moving forward on my new path. Your belief in my future success and me is priceless.

To Jim Kelley: Thank you for giving me a chance to spread my wings and enter the sales side of banking. You believed in me even when those around you doubted your decision and questioned your approval of my new sales position. Had you not allowed me to make the change, I wouldn't be living this amazing life. So many corporate leaders only think about what's best for the company; you thought about what was best for me. I thank you from the bottom of my heart. I'll be forever grateful to you.

To Jennifer Myers, Swan Design: Your creativity never ceases to amaze me. The contributions you've made to this book through your design work are fantastic. You have such a great vision and an incredible skill that pinpoints exactly what I'm looking for. I appreciate all you've done for me. You're the best.

To Adrienne Moch: You have such a passion for writing and editing. You're a consummate professional. I love your no nonsense style and how you get down to business. You truly care about the English language and how it's written. You care about the writer and the reader. Thanks for your expertise and professionalism. You're an amazing editor.

TABLE OF CONTENTS

INTRODUCTION

IF FOLLOW UP IS SO IMPORTANT...
WHY DON'T YOU CONSISTENTLY DO IT?

Whether you're a salesperson, business owner or customer service representative, I have no doubt you know how important follow up is...so why don't you consistently do it? I have a few theories:

1. You don't think you have the time.

2. You don't know the best way to follow up with prospects and clients.

3. You don't have a good system to support your follow-up efforts.

These mindsets and the lack of good follow-up habits will create holes in your client base and prospecting pipeline, leaving them vulnerable to your competition. To self-assess your follow-up behavior, answer the following questions:

1. Do you stay in touch with your clients and prospects as often as you should?

2. Have you ever had a prospect and/or client ask you to call them back at a later date and you didn't?

3. Have you needed to get back to a prospect, but couldn't find his information or remember exactly what took place during your conversation?

4. Have you ever been embarrassed by your lack of follow up?

5. Have you ever been in a time of need and too embarrassed to call those who can help because you haven't stayed in touch?

6. Have you ever felt you've been neglectful of your clients and prospects?

7. Does follow up get the same priority as checking your email, voice mail and social media sites?

It's obvious what the answers should be to these questions. However, not being able to answer them correctly is exactly why most people need to work on their follow-up skills.

Follow up is a key ingredient to success and there's so much depth to it. It goes way beyond just getting back to someone when you say you will. Your clients, prospects and referral sources should **never** stop hearing from you; follow up is something you should do forever.

In my opinion, and for the purposes of this book, follow up is synonymous with staying in touch. I'll use these two terms interchangeably because they're one in the same. Other terms I'll use to reflect follow up are reaching out, touches and touch point.

While reading this book, there may be times when you squirm, cringe or maybe even get embarrassed because of your inconsistent follow-up habits. Don't worry; I'll give you ideas, tips and suggestions on how to turn things around and be proud and confident in your follow-up behavior and practices.

I've done many speaking engagements on this topic and what I've learned from audience members is they really do want to be better in the area of follow up. They understand its importance, but they just don't know how to do it effectively.

By implementing the seven principles outlined in this book and completing the Get the Ball Rolling Action Steps, you'll take a huge step toward developing and implementing a good follow-up system. You'll become skilled at creating and retaining relationships that are important to you, and you'll also rid yourself of the burden of guilt, embarrassment, and discomfort from your lack of follow up. These negative emotions will be replaced with positive ones, such as appreciation, confidence and comfort. My Follow Up Savvy System will clear the way for you to enjoy an elevated level of success.

If you're open to learning, and committed to making changes and being better at follow up, let's get the ball rolling.

Why I Wrote This Book

I was a business banker for 25 years, specializing in SBA lending. For 20 of those 25 years, I was involved in the operations side of the SBA process. SBA loans are laden with rules and regulations. I learned early on that to keep compliant with all the rules and regulations, solid systems and procedures needed to be in place. As an SBA manager, I was responsible for my departments being compliant. Because of this experience, I developed a forte for creating systems.

My last five years in banking were spent in business development and branch management. I went to many sales training classes and got a clear understanding of how being good at follow up could increase my chances of success. I took my skills and understanding of creating systems and applied them to my follow-up efforts. By the time I left banking, I'd established the solid follow-up system that I share with you in this book: the Follow Up Savvy System. I've achieved successes that wouldn't have been possible with out this system in place, some of which appear on these pages.

The last bank I worked for was acquired, and on the day the merger closed, the senior management team, which included me, was let go. I chose not to stay in banking and became a distributor with SendOutCards. When I changed careers, I put the Follow Up Savvy System to the first of numerous tests. I needed to notify all my banking clients, prospects, referral sources and colleagues of my career change, and I also wanted to approach them about looking at the SendOutCards program. Because I had a follow-up system in place, I was able to very comfortably contact everyone in my database. This was my time of need and I didn't have one moment of awkwardness about approaching anyone from my past.

Since implementing this follow-up system, I've received many compliments on my follow-up efforts. In addition, I've also been asked a lot of questions about my system, including how I stay on top of my calls, not lose track of anyone, and stay organized to the point of never forgetting anyone's birthday. After being asked these questions so many times, I realized I needed to share my system.

I put together a presentation on the importance of follow up and how being good at it can be very powerful. I started speaking to sales teams and business organizations. When I give my presentations, I don't cover all seven principles for timing reasons; I generally cover one to three of them. Regardless of the amount of time I have to speak or how many principles I cover, the response I get from audience members is overwhelming. They're like sponges, drinking up everything I present and suggest. I hear comments like, "I hope I wrote everything down," "I'd love to hear more on this subject," and "I really needed to hear this information."

It was during those moments when I realized I needed to write a book and get the information in a form that audience members could take with them. Additionally, those who couldn't attend a presentation or workshop could have the information available to them in book form. I thank my audience members for their great feedback, which inspired me to write this book.

As I share my real-life experiences with you, I'll reference "my program," "my card program" and "the program" throughout the book. In all instances, I'm referring to the SendOutCards program.

I live in the sales world every day. I share my experiences, victories and successes in the hope they'll inspire and motivate you to improve your follow-up habits.

PRINCIPLE 1:

3 RESULTS OF EFFECTIVE FOLLOW UP

Why is being good at follow up so important? If you really look at success, doesn't it boil down to relationships? Yes, you have to be good at what you do and knowledgeable about your products or services, but that's not an ironclad reason for someone to do business with you. You also have to have good relationships. I'm sure you've heard the saying, people do business with people they know, like and trust. If someone's going to have a chance at getting to know you, like you and trust you, you have to stay in touch and work the relationship. Once you're known, liked and trusted, getting business will be much easier.

"You get back what you send out" and "you reap what you sow" are universal adages that are very applicable to follow up. When you show people you care about them, it's human nature for them to want to help you. This help can come in many forms, including more business, referrals, time and opportunity.

When you're reaching out, staying in touch and following up, be sure you're genuine. Your efforts should come from the place of caring and truly wanting the relationship. Stay in touch because you care for people, you appreciate them and you want to strengthen relationships. Don't make gestures of staying in touch if you're only doing it to *get* something; you'll come across as insincere and self-serving. Being authentic is a must.

Effective follow up can have any number of great results, but in this principle we focus on three:

- Strengthening relationships

- Creating loyalty

- Becoming referable

Let's take an in-depth look at these three desired follow-up results.

Result #1
You'll strengthen your relationships.

It's impossible to have a good relationship with someone if you're not staying in touch. By losing touch, the quality of your relationships will weaken. Relationships are like plants; they must be nurtured and cared for. If they're left untended, they'll wither away and die.

Here are some indicators of a strong relationship:

1. You're comfortable picking the phone up and calling at any time and for any reason

2. You stay in touch a minimum of three to four times a year

3. You have verbal communication over the phone or in person a minimum of two times a year

4. You remember important dates and occasions

When you've implemented the Follow Up Savvy System, you'll stay in touch with your clients, prospects and referral sources a minimum of four times per year. You'll stay in touch with your business associates and competitors a minimum of three times per year. By the end of this book, you'll have plenty of ideas how to do that. You'll see that it's not as burdensome as it may sound.

Plan your three/four touches around the person's birthday. For example, if a client's birthday is January 1, you'll touch her on that day. The other three touches will be in April, July and October. If you're touching an associate or competitor three times a year and his birthday is in August, you'll touch him in August, December and April.

How you touch them each time will vary, with the exception of birthdays. Always send a birthday card and possibly a gift, depending on the relationship. You'll make a birthday call as well. This is discussed in more detail in Principle 4. The other touches throughout the year should include at least one phone call or an in-person meeting; you want to make sure to talk to everyone in your database at least twice a year.

What you do for the other one or two touches will depend on what feels right that day and what other touches you've made. Your touches should vary from phone calls, emails and cards to lunch and coffee meetings. If you interact with someone in your database between your designated months to reach out, don't change the schedule; just chalk it up to touching that person more than three or four times that year.

All it takes to stay on top of these touches is a good reminder system. I'll discuss this in more detail in Principle 3. When you're consistently staying in touch, you're guaranteed to have better and stronger relationships.

The relationships you need to nurture may go beyond the decision maker. Don't forget about office managers, bookkeepers, administrative assistants, personal assistants and anyone else who's tied closely to the decision maker. In many instances, these "right-hand" folks have a lot of influence. Treat them as if they're clients.

It may have struck you as odd that I suggest staying in touch with your competitors, but if you have a genuine connection with them, you should want to develop a relationship. Competitors can also be good referral sources.

When I was a banker, it wasn't uncommon for me to get a call from one of my competitor friends who had a loan his bank wouldn't approve. He'd call me to see if I'd look at the deal. Every bank has its own criteria and what doesn't work for one can be a great fit for another, so inter-bank referrals were a great source of business.

Now that I'm out of banking, those who were once my competitors aren't any longer; they're now prospects for my SendOutCards business. Because someone is a competitor today, doesn't mean she always will be. When I left banking, I was grateful I'd nurtured relationships with my competitor friends. It makes it very easy for me to approach them about my card program because I've consistently stayed in touch with them and invested time into the relationship.

What if a competitor friend gets out of the industry and is looking for someone to whom he can refer clients and prospects? If you've nurtured that relationship and he knows you care, you could be the beneficiary of those great referrals.

Can you see why you shouldn't rule out befriending your competition?

We live in an electronic world that's filled with emails, online newsletters, social media, blogging, etc. These are important means of communication, but you shouldn't rely solely on them. It can appear impersonal, plus it's much harder to strengthen relationships online.

Case in Point #1

I used to work with a woman named Ann. She left the bank approximately seven years ago. I lost touch with her, as did other staff members. (This was in my pre-Follow Up Savvy System days.) She recently showed up on one of the social media sites and we connected. I asked her if she wanted to get together for coffee. We met and had a great time updating each other on what's gone on in our lives over the last seven years.

A few days later, I ran into another woman, Kim, who also worked with Ann and me at the bank. Kim told me she connected with Ann through the social media site and noted that Ann wasn't married. That was the only information Kim had on Ann. I told her Ann and I met for coffee and not only was she unmarried, but she just bought a house that she's renting out, she's thinking about starting a business on the side, she loves her job in property management, she and her mom went to a great three-day health seminar in Orange County, and she's as beautiful as she was seven years ago.

For Kim to get this much information electronically, there would have been a lot of back and forth and it might have taken days or weeks to cover what Ann and I covered in one hour over coffee. I ask you, who had the better connection with Ann, Kim or me? The answer is obvious.

Case in Point #2

I've been going to my hairdresser, Joni, for 10 years. She's one of the happiest and friendliest people I know. She always makes me feel like she's so excited to see me, and I've never seen her in a down mood. Joni is always upbeat, laughing and friendly. She's a great example of a provider of first class service, which is discussed in Principle 5.

On my last visit, Joni told me that Karen, a fellow stylist, is moving out of state and wants to refer clients to her. Karen told Joni she's watched how Joni interacts with her clients and was so impressed that she wants her clients going to Joni. There are five other stylists in the salon, but Joni was Karen's choice to get her referrals.

What's the moral to this story? When you're in a business setting, everything you do is leaving an impression and you never know who's watching or what opportunities will come your way. Karen was once a competitor of Joni's and in the blink of an eye, she turned into a referral source. Joni's client base (and income) increased immediately.

Result #2
You'll create client and prospect loyalty.

We all want loyal clients and prospects, but that doesn't happen without a concerted effort. You must **CREATE** the loyalty and make sure it's maintained. Since clients and prospects require slightly different approaches, let's look at them one at a time.

Client Loyalty

A by-product of client loyalty is a great level of comfort and confidence. When you have loyalty, your client base isn't vulnerable to your competition.

Are you giddy when you get the news that a prospect has chosen to do business with you? Do you court your prospects through the prospecting phase, woo them during the closing phase and then forget about them after business has been done? Once business has been transacted, are you off looking for your next new client and forgetting about those who have already done business with you?

Your clients can be a great resource for you. They've experienced your products or services and they know what kind of customer service you provide. If they've had a pleasant experience, make sure they don't forget about you. Instead of running around looking for new prospects, think about cultivating people with whom you already have relationships.

It's been said that the average person knows 250 people. Assuming you know 250 people, what if each of those 250 would refer you to just one person from his or her 250 people? Even if we're more conservative and cut that in half, so 125 of those 250 referred you to just one person…imagine what that would do for your business.

Remember that you must have a good relationship with someone before he'll be willing to refer you and share his contacts with you. Wouldn't it make sense to spend some of your time with current and past clients and continue to nurture those relationships? I'll give you ideas in Principle 4 about how to stay in touch after business has been conducted.

Don't lose the excitement and appreciation for your clients, current and past. You should always hold them in the same regard as you did when they were new. They deserve this. The last thing you want to do is take them for granted.

Being good is not a good enough reason for your clients to be loyal to you. Being good is expected. People aren't going to decide to do business with you if they think you might be substandard. Don't rest in the thought that "my client is happy with me and/or my product/service, so he'll remember me and remain loyal." If clients don't hear from you consistently and know you care beyond business reasons, loyalty will be hard to come by.

If you're in a transactional business, you're in more danger of losing client loyalty if you're not staying in touch. Don't think, "I've already done business with her so she won't need my services again." This is foolish. Clients may not need your services any time soon or possibly ever again, but they may know someone who will.

Case in Point #1

Four years ago, my husband and father each bought a car, in the same week, from Ted, the same auto broker. Ted was a delight to work with. He was professional and knowledgeable, and made the process of buying a car very pleasant for both my father and husband. I ran into Ted six months ago and asked him if we could get together and catch up.

During our meeting, I realized if I'd known anyone who was buying or selling a car over the last four years, I wouldn't have thought to refer Ted. For a moment, I was perplexed. It didn't make any sense for me not to think of Ted because he was very good and we were very happy with his services. Then, it dawned on me that we hadn't heard from Ted since the day we walked out of his office, four years ago, with the keys to our new car.

To make this story even more telling, there's a restaurant in the same center as Ted's office that my husband and I frequent probably once a month. I still never thought of Ted. This story shows how being good is not a good enough reason for people to remember you. Everyone is busy, so it's up to you to make sure you're not forgotten.

Case in Point #2

I've gone to the same eye doctor's office for the last 13 years; it's a couple of miles from my home, making it very convenient. Eight years ago, the doctor sold the practice. I decided to continue going there and gave the new doctor a try. I'll call her Dr. J. She was very nice, she appeared knowledgeable and the service was good. I go for my annual eye exam and get a one-year prescription for contacts. It's very easy for me to know when I'm due for my annual exam; when the contacts run low, it's time to call for an appointment.

When it came time to make the call for my second annual appointment with the new doctor, I couldn't remember her name. I realized I'd not heard from her since my last appointment, one year ago, so nothing had prompted me to remember it. Fortunately, I have all my doctors organized in my database and when I pulled up the list of names, I knew she'd be the one I didn't recognize. I found Dr. J's number and scheduled my next appointment. Again, she was very nice, she was good and I had no complaints. When it came time for my third annual appointment, I received a letter in the mail reminding me to get scheduled. Dr. J had obviously implemented a system to send reminder appointment letters, her one and only annual communication. If that letter got lost in the mail or was accidentally thrown away, I wouldn't hear from her office at all.

For the last five years, I've continued to go to Dr. J out of sheer convenience. I can't say I have a relationship with her because I merely see her once a year to get an exam and a new prescription for my contacts. During my last visit, she told me she's moving the office to a new location approximately 10 miles from where I live. I'm not interested in driving to her new location. I'm not attached to her, have no loyalty and really don't have a relationship. I want to reiterate that Dr. J is good and nice, but that's not enough to make me want to drive to her new office. I'll begin looking for a new eye doctor closer to my home.

Over the last five years, since Dr. J bought the practice, she's put no effort into creating patient loyalty. By not staying in touch and reaching out in any way other than annual reminder letters, she's made herself vulnerable to losing patients like me.

Case in Point #3

I bought my condo 13 years ago. The realtor was great; she was nice, knowledgeable about the area I was looking to buy in and very responsive to my requests. I would have been more than happy to refer her to anyone I knew who had a need for a realtor. Unfortunately, after escrow closed, I never heard from her again. I don't remember her name and I wouldn't know her if she was standing in front of me.

Being good is not a good enough reason for your clients to stay with you or remember you. Give them a better reason.

Prospect Loyalty

Yes, it's possible to create prospect loyalty. Often, when prospects tell you no, that means they're just not ready. A prospect may not be ready to do business with you because of timing, cost or inconvenience, but life and circumstances change daily. What used to be the wrong time, too much or too inconvenient may no longer be the case. It's imperative that you consistently stay in touch with your prospects so when their circumstances change, you'll be the person they call. You want to be the first person they think of when they're ready to take action.

Start treating your prospects as if they're already clients. You can make great strides in developing prospect loyalty by remembering them on their birthday, sending holiday cards and checking in a couple times a year to see how they're doing. Your contact doesn't even have to end when a prospect tells you he's not interested in your product or service or he's going to do business with one of your competitors. Always be respectful of his decision. Let him know you appreciate the time he's given you and you enjoyed getting to know him. End the conversation by asking if it would be OK to stay in periodic touch. I've never had anyone tell me no.

Case in Point

One of my prospects, Steve, hasn't yet had a need for my card program and we've been in the prospecting phase for two years. He recently told me one of my competitors talked to him about the card program. Steve told my competitor that when he's ready to sign up, he's going to go with me. Steve is loyal to me because I've consistently stayed in touch with him over the last two years by remembering him on his birthday, sending holiday cards, making Just Because Calls (discussed in Principle 4) *and* we've had lunch. I've been treating him as if he was already a client, which has created prospect loyalty.

Result #3
You'll become referable.

This is the grand prize from a prospecting point of view. When you've put forth the efforts that have resulted in strengthening your relationships and creating loyalty, you've now become referable. Referrals are the easiest leads you'll ever get. You have someone out there selling you and your products or services on your behalf. Your referral sources are comfortable referring you because you've proven your ability to take care of relationships and they're confident you'll handle their referrals in the same way you handle your relationship with them.

I'd venture to say that everyone in business would love to have their lead generation be referral based. It cuts down on time and cost to close business, while increasing your likelihood of making the sale. When you meet a prospect at a networking event, it takes time to get to know that person and more importantly, for her to get to know you and your company, products or services. When a prospect is referred, most likely the person referring her has given you an approval rating, so you're much further ahead in the prospecting phase than if you were dealing with a cold prospect.

 ## "Get The Ball Rolling" Action Steps

How should you get started down the road to getting the three results you want from your follow-up efforts?

1. List your top 20 clients.

2. List your top 20 prospects.

3. List your top 20 referral sources, vendors or anyone else who supports your business.

4. Next to each name, write down the last time you had verbal communication with that person over the phone or in person.

5. In the final column, put down another date as a commitment to contact the person within the next 30 days. If you contact three of the 60 names per day, you'll be done in one month.

6. Review this list of 60 and ask yourself the following questions:

    a. "Would my competition like to have these people?"

    b. "What am I doing to strengthen my relationship with each person to protect them from my competition?"

    c. When was the last time I did something special for these people?

When writing down your top 20 clients, keep your past clients in mind. You may have landed their business when you were with another company. That's OK; write them down. This will be a good time to reconnect. When writing down your top 20 prospects, keep in mind those who've told you no or chose to go with a competitor.

This list of 60 is your crème de la crème. **Take exceptional care of them!**

Once you've completed your top 20 in each category, you can go on to the next 20 and the next 20 and so on.

<u>TOP 20 CLIENTS</u>

<u>Name</u>	**Date of Last <u>Verbal Communication</u>**	**Date I Will <u>Contact Them</u>**
1) _____	_____	_____
2) _____	_____	_____
3) _____	_____	_____
4) _____	_____	_____
5) _____	_____	_____
6) _____	_____	_____
7) _____	_____	_____
8) _____	_____	_____
9) _____	_____	_____
10) _____	_____	_____
11) _____	_____	_____
12) _____	_____	_____
13) _____	_____	_____
14) _____	_____	_____
15) _____	_____	_____
16) _____	_____	_____
17) _____	_____	_____
18) _____	_____	_____
19) _____	_____	_____
20) _____	_____	_____

Wanda Allen

TOP 20 PROSPECTS

	Name	Date of Last Verbal Communication	Date I Will Contact Them
1)			
2)			
3)			
4)			
5)			
6)			
7)			
8)			
9)			
10)			
11)			
12)			
13)			
14)			
15)			
16)			
17)			
18)			
19)			
20)			

TOP 20 REFERRAL SOURCES, VENDORS OR
ANYONE ELSE WHO SUPPORTS YOUR BUSINESS

<u>Name</u>	Date of Last <u>Verbal Communication</u>	Date I Will <u>Contact Them</u>
1) _____	_____	_____
2) _____	_____	_____
3) _____	_____	_____
4) _____	_____	_____
5) _____	_____	_____
6) _____	_____	_____
7) _____	_____	_____
8) _____	_____	_____
9) _____	_____	_____
10) _____	_____	_____
11) _____	_____	_____
12) _____	_____	_____
13) _____	_____	_____
14) _____	_____	_____
15) _____	_____	_____
16) _____	_____	_____
17) _____	_____	_____
18) _____	_____	_____
19) _____	_____	_____
20) _____	_____	_____

PRINCIPLE 2:

GET ORGANIZED

If you're sitting there rolling your eyes, thinking, "not the get organized lecture," I'm sorry to disappoint you. The more organized you are, the easier it's going to be to stay on top of your follow up.

Do you have mounds of paper sitting on your desk? Is your filing out of control? Is your in-basket in overload? Do you have stacks of business cards from people you've met and haven't done anything with? If you answered yes to one or all of these questions, you need to get some organization in place and get some systems set up.

One of the main problems with disorganization is it's a time killer. When you're organized, you don't waste time on nonsense such as sifting through piles of paper, looking for reports, trying to find contact information for someone you need to call, locating your keys, and remembering previous conversations. If you're unorganized, it appears that you have too much going on and you're having trouble keeping everything in order.

According to Thesauras.com, synonyms for unorganized are all over the place, chaotic, cluttered, confused, dislocated, disordered, jumbled, messed up, messy, mixed up, scattered, scrambled, sloppy, unarranged, unkempt, unsystematic, and untidy. None of those is very becoming. If you appear to be unorganized, you run the risk of your clients, prospects, referral sources and anyone else perceiving you in any one of these negative ways. On the flip side, one of the definitions of organized, according to Thesauras.com, is systematized. This one word encapsulates the point of this entire book. Your follow-up efforts **must** be systematized to be effective.

When I was a banker, I saw and managed my share of both organized and unorganized people. It's so common to hear an unorganized person say things like:

- I can't be organized.

- I don't have time to be organized.

- This is just the way I am.

- My desk may look like a mess, but I know where everything is.

They believe these statements wholeheartedly. What about you? Be careful if you find yourself justifying your unorganized ways with these kinds of thoughts. They can turn into a false sense that being disorganized is OK. Disorganization can have an adverse effect on your success and make it more difficult than it needs to be.

It's been said that first impressions are made between the first seven to 30 seconds. Right or wrong, when someone meets you for the first time, she forms an opinion of you in those first impression moments. These judgments are made based on what's seen and said, including personal appearance, your smile, the tone of your voice, how or if you make eye contact, your handshake, and even the condition of your desk. You won't get a second chance for a first impression, so use those initial seconds wisely. Impressions continue to be made based on your actions, such as whether you're on time for appointments, you follow up when you say you will, you're knowledgeable about your products or services, and your car is in good condition. You might be thinking, "what does my car have to do with anything?" If there's ever a chance a client, prospect or referral source will ride in your car, make sure you don't need a few minutes to clear out the passenger seat.

I'm sure you know people who are always running around with "their hair on fire." This is another sign of disorganization. These are the people who'll tell you how busy they are and why they aren't getting things done. They'll tell you everything going on in their life that's made it difficult for them to return phone calls and emails, prospect, close business and whatever else they're responsible for getting done that hasn't happened.

This gives the appearance that they may not have room for any more business, because they're having a hard time keeping up with what they already have. This is not a good impression. We all have crazy days, weeks or even months, but be careful about sharing this information. If you're out of sorts, does it really need to be publicly known? You risk losing confidence with prospects, clients and referral sources. Everything you say and do leaves an impression. Be sure you're doing what you can to leave a good one.

The key to getting and staying organized is to establish good habits and make them non- negotiable. If you need help in this area, there are many books on time management and organization. You can also consider hiring a professional organizer or a business coach to help you create habits and systems that will work for you.

Case in Point

My husband and I hired an attorney, Joe, several years ago. He came highly recommended by a friend of my husband's who's also an attorney. My husband's friend didn't practice law in the area we needed, which is why he referred us to Joe. When we went to Joe's office for our first meeting, he was almost 30 minutes late. I wasn't happy from the start, because I'd taken time off work and needed to get back to the office.

When we went into his office, it was an absolute mess. He had piles of papers all over his desk and on the floor. I wondered where *our* pile of papers would go in this mess. My first impression was not good, to say the least. I gave my husband a look that clearly showed I wasn't impressed.

At the end of the meeting, it came time to write Joe a check for the retainer fee. I wrote it very hesitantly, but my husband assured me, because he was so highly recommended by his friend, that everything would be fine. The check was sizeable and I needed to transfer money from another account to cover it, but I wasn't going to be able to make the transfer until the following day. I asked Joe to hold the check for one day before he deposited it. He agreed, but he then deposited it the day I gave it to him and the check bounced. I was upset because he didn't follow through on holding the check a day, so I had to deal with overdraft fees.

The next call was to my husband. I reiterated my concern about using Joe's services. Once again, my husband reassured me that Joe was an expert in his field of law and everything would be OK. From that point on, dealing with Joe was a horrible experience. He never met deadlines, never called when he said he would and rarely returned our phone calls. In fact, we had so many unreturned phone calls, my husband had to go to Joe's office numerous times to get updates on our case. I look back and say to myself "I should have walked on that first day and never wrote him a check." The fact that he was 30 minutes late and the condition of his desk were enough warning signs for me. I'll never go against my intuition again.

"Get The Ball Rolling" Action Steps

"Rome wasn't built in a day," so if you've been disorganized for some time, you won't be able to magically snap your fingers and turn things around…but you need to start somewhere.

1. Organize your desk. Clear the clutter.

2. Get caught up on your filing

3. Organize your car. Make it presentable to anyone who needs to ride with you.

4. If you want help in this area, contact a professional organizer or business coach.

PRINCIPLE 3:

WHY A RELIABLE DATABASE IS CRITICAL TO YOUR FOLLOW-UP SYSTEM

It's very important to have a database that's easy to use, accessible when you need it, and effective at tracking and helping you execute tasks that need to be done. Whatever system you use, it must be simple. If it's too cumbersome, it becomes a burden rather than an asset.

If you're on a complicated system, ask yourself if all the information it contains is necessary. If not, then use only what is. You'll also want to be careful about not using too many programs. If you have to go into multiple programs, it can become burdensome and time-consuming, which might deter you from using them at all.

Find a program that works best for you, implement it and use it without fail. Whatever system you use, be sure you consistently update it and make it your #1 follow-up tool. You can have the best program in existence, but if you don't develop a habit of using it, it doesn't do you any good.

A good system will make it easy for you to track important dates and organize your contacts. It should also have a reminder system and a good notes section where you can document all your touches and conversations. This does two things: 1) it will help you strategize your next touch and 2) it makes you look very good to the person you're touching. It shows you remember previous conversations and/or touches and are paying attention to details. This will go a long way in making a good impression.

If you already have a database program, go through it and make sure your contact information for each person is current. Get rid of any contacts who are no longer good or ones with whom you don't want to stay in touch. Having a clean and up-to-date database is an important part of getting organized. You want to feel good about the contacts you have in your program.

There are two schools of thought on building your database. One is that you should have as many contacts as possible. Everyone you meet, regardless of your connection with them, should go in; if you have a business card, put that person in. I know people who have thousands of names in their database.

For the purposes of this book, I operate out of the other school of thought, which is only enter contacts into your database when you have a true connection with them and are interested in establishing a relationship. It's hard to manage and stay in touch with thousands of people unless you're doing so electronically, with emails, newsletters, etc. If you're set on building a database of "the masses," be sure your program has a feature that allows you to organize your contacts. This way, you can separate the more meaningful relationships, such as clients, prospects, referral sources, vendors, etc.

 ## Case in Point

The last bank I worked at had a database program with a lot of bells and whistles, but no one knew how to use all the features. It was too complicated, we never got proper training and it was inconvenient. My usage became very haphazard.

I went to a networking event and my name was pulled in a raffle; I won the opportunity to send out two free greeting cards on a program called SendOutCards. I was so impressed at how easy it was to send the cards that I signed up for the program.

I subsequently realized the program had a database component to it. After using SendOutCards for a few weeks, I decided to discontinue my use of the bank's program and use SendOutCards as my sole database program. It tracks important dates, I can organize my contacts, and it has a reminder system and a good notes section.

Because the bank's system was so complicated, the simplicity of SendOutCards was very appealing to me. I love the fact that it's a web-based program. This means I have access to it anywhere I am as long as I can get on the Internet. To use the bank's system, I had to be in the bank. I also love the idea that I can easily send out cards and gifts, which are a couple of ways I stay in touch. This system keeps me organized and on top of my follow- up responsibilities. To learn more about the SendOutCards program, go to www.sendoutcards.com/wandascards.

"Get The Ball Rolling" Action Steps

Since your database is going to drive your follow-up activities, Principle 3 is especially critical.

1. Decide on a database program that's right for you.

2. Input your contacts.

3. If you have a database program, review your contacts and do any necessary cleanup, such as removing names and updating contact information.

4. If you have a stack of business cards on your desk, go through them and do one of the following:

    a. Input the contact information into your database

    b. Throw away the card

The thought of throwing a business card away may make you uncomfortable. My logic behind this is if you've had the card for any length of time and haven't done anything with it, what are the chances you'll do something with it in the future? It will likely remain as clutter on your desk. If someone isn't worthy of being put in your database, why keep the card?

You might also wonder whether you should keep the business card of those people who are in your database. If they're people you refer, I suggest putting their cards in a business card holder and keeping it in your car. This way, as you're out and about, you'll have the cards with you when opportunities arise to make referrals. If they're not people you refer, why keep their business card once they are in your database?

PRINCIPLE 4:

9 WAYS TO STAY IN TOUCH YEAR IN AND YEAR OUT

I hope you're starting to get a good understanding of the benefits and success you can experience through good follow-up habits. You may be thinking, OK, I understand how important it is, but how do I go about doing it? This principle will answer that question.

The Follow Up Savvy System includes nine different ways for you to stay in touch and consistently follow up. In Principle 1, Result 3, Action Step 6, you were asked to think about what special thing you've done for your Top 60. These nine ways will give you some ideas on what that something special can be.

It's very important to be sure that the touches you choose to make fit into your schedule and budget. If you have a small client, that special touch may be a phone call or coffee meeting. For your bigger clients, it may be dinner, tickets to a ball game or an annual lunch at their favorite restaurant. All nine ways may not resonate with you. That's OK; choose the ones that do.

If you like all nine, that's great, but understand it will take some time to implement them; be patient and don't try to do all of them at once. That would be like deciding to live a healthier life and committing to exercising five days a week, drinking eight glasses of water a day, giving up sugar and no longer drinking alcohol…all at the same time. You'd be setting yourself up for failure, since you're trying to do too much at one time. The same goes here. Don't get overly excited and try all the follow-up methods at once, have it become overwhelming, and then end up doing none of them. Implement these ideas one at time. Get good at one, and then move onto the next. For some of these, there will be an information-gathering process that will take some time.

Method #1

Nice To Meet You

Do you go to networking events, make some great contacts, collect business cards and then do nothing with them other than add them to the existing stack of business cards on your desk? If you're not doing anything with the new contacts you make, putting forth whatever effort you did to make them will go to waste. You'll get the same result as if you never met the person.

Networking isn't cheap and it takes time, so to do nothing with the contacts you make at events is a waste of precious time and money. One part of getting organized is doing something with all those business cards and making sure you don't let them pile up again. This was addressed in Principles 2 and 3.

With the Follow Up Savvy System, you'll reach out to new contacts promptly, naturally eliminating the buildup of business cards. After you make a true connection with someone, send that person a nice-to-meet-you card, give him a call, schedule a coffee meeting, or email him and set up a follow-up meeting. Make an effort to establish a relationship. Find out what his needs are and how you can help him; your goal is to make yourself valuable.

When you send your nice-to-meet-you message, don't mention your business, which can appear to be self-serving. Be interested in your new contact and his business. As you establish the relationship, you'll have plenty of opportunity to discuss your business.

Making a true connection with someone involves more than spending a couple minutes with him, getting his business card, putting him on your distribution email list or requesting a connection with him on a social media site. These methods may be part of your efforts to touch new contacts, but as I noted previously, you shouldn't rely solely on electronic means. By doing so, you're reaching out on a superficial level and it won't set you apart.

Get your nice-to-meet-you message out no later than 48 hours after meeting someone. If much more time goes by, you may not get it out at all, or if you do, you may feel a little embarrassed if too much time has passed by.

Case in Point

I went to a networking event and met an architect, Kit, who specializes in high-end properties. I enjoyed hearing about her background and learning about her business. During our conversation, I thought of two people I know who might be good referral sources for her; one is a landscape designer who works only on high-end properties and the other is an interior designer. I asked Kit if these two would be people she'd be interested in meeting, and she said yes.

The next day, I got my nice-to-meet-you card out to Kit and then called the landscape designer and interior designer. They were both interested in meeting Kit and gave me their permission to hand out their contact information.

I never refer people and distribute their contact information without first getting their permission. This allows me to warm up the referral and make sure they're interested. Kit will have a better chance of success with these two people because I've contacted them.

When I called Kit with the referrals, she told me she'd received my nice-to-meet-you card. She expressed appreciation for both the card and the referrals. She also said she was interested in talking to me about my card program and wanted to set up a time for a demo.

If you've been following closely, you'll realize I hadn't asked Kit if she was interested in seeing a demo. Rather than focusing on my business and me, I was focused on helping her, but I ended booking a demo in the very early stage of our relationship. This is what can happen when you reach out and genuinely try to help others. Remember, what you send out comes back.

"Get The Ball Rolling" Action Steps

Differentiate yourself by doing more than merely establishing an electronic connection…or failing to follow up at all.

1. Commit to reaching out to your new contacts within 48 hours and determine how you'll reach out.

2. If you've met someone in the last week and haven't reached out – commit to doing it today.

Methods 2, 3 and 4 all involve saying thank you. It's crazy to think that saying thank you will make you stand out and be different, but it does…because so few people do it. Many people have convinced themselves they're too busy for even the most common of courtesies.

If you're not in the habit of saying thank you, know that it's never too late. Not saying thank you can leave a very bad impression and make you appear unappreciative. If you're late with it, just admit it. Begin by apologizing for taking so long to say thank you and carry on with the rest of your message. You'll gain far more credibility with a late thank you than you will with none at all.

Method #2

Thank You For Your Business

This may seem obvious, but it's sad to say that many people don't thank their clients for their business. Ask yourself, "of the people who I do business with, who's thanked me"? Think about your banker, realtor, hairdresser, dry cleaners, dentist, optometrist and so on. I'd venture to say that most have not thanked you for being a client or patient. Now, let me flip that question around: how many clients have you thanked?

The size of your thank you will vary depending on the size of your client and your budget. Regardless of how small a client is, never forget to say thank you. Small clients can grow into big ones, and they may also know people who could be large clients. Even your smallest clients have agreed to pay for your product or service, so they deserve a thank you. Get your thank you out within 24 hours of transacting business.

Case in Point

I send a thank you card and brownies to every client who signs up for my card program. I tell clients I appreciate their business and am honored to have them as clients, and I let them know I look forward to working with them. This is such a simple gesture, but the response is incredible. It really does make people feel appreciated.

"Get The Ball Rolling" Action Steps

It doesn't take much to become a "thank you for your business" machine:

1. Print out a list of all your current clients. If you haven't thanked them, commit to doing so within the next 30 days. It doesn't matter how long they've been a client. Again, a late thank you is better than none at all.

2. For future new clients, commit to thanking them within 24 hours after business has been transacted.

3. Decide what your thank you will consist of based on the size of the relationship and your budget.

Method #3

Thank You For The Referral

As previously mentioned, referrals are the easiest leads you'll ever get. You have someone out there selling you and your products or services on your behalf. It's crucial that you take care of your referral sources. When I get a referral, I send a thank you card with a $5 Starbucks card to the referral source, regardless of what happens with the referral. If I end up transacting business, I send another thank you card with a larger gift or I may take the referrer to lunch or dinner. The gift varies depending on the size of business that was transacted.

When you get a referral, be sure to keep the referrer updated on its status. Have you ever given a referral to someone and then found yourself wondering what happened? Don't let your referral sources ask that same question of you. Make a note to always update the referrer when you have any type of communication with the referral. This is another way to show you appreciate the referral and you're staying on top of it. It also shows your referral sources that you're not forgetting about them.

Case in Point

I referred a friend to an associate. Business was conducted several times over a two- month period, but I never heard from my associate. Not a thank you email, call or card. I'm sure she was appreciative of the referral, but it appears she wasn't. I found myself wondering if she really thinks she's so busy that she can't even call or email a thank you…and questioning whether I'd refer her again. I prefer to refer business to people who show their appreciation, because that could be a reflection of how they handle their relationships in general.

"Get The Ball Rolling" Action Steps

Since so many people fail to thank their referral sources, you can really stand out when you implement this simple, yet powerful action.

1. Set up a timeline for getting thank yous out to your referral sources.

2. Decide how you'll thank your referral sources, i.e. calls, emails, cards and/or gifts.

3. List all the referrals you've received in the last six months that turned into closed business. Commit to getting a thank you out to those referral sources within the next week, if you haven't already done so.

Method #4

Thank You For Your Time

When people give you their time, it's important to thank them. This may be a prospect who agreed to meet with you, a client who's looking for additional services, a referral source who agreed to hear about a new product you're offering or someone who's volunteered her time for a cause for you. There may be many other reasons someone has given you their time, and a thank you is appropriate for them all.

 ## Case in Point #1

I have a client who works for a university in San Diego. I belong to a women's networking group that supported her university's scholarship program. She sent me a card thanking me for the time I'd invested in the program, showing me how appreciative she was. I'd be more than happy to help her again.

Case in Point #2

A colleague was asked by someone she knows professionally to participate in a fundraiser by doing a 30-minute presentation as part of a lengthier event. She was happy to do it, since she believes in the cause and likes the person who made the request. She worked hard on the presentation and prepared handouts to add value for the attendees. Everything went great at the event, but to this very day, she's not received a thank you from the person who requested her participation. That oversight will give her pause for thought if she's asked to do something like that again by the same person.

"Get The Ball Rolling" Action Steps

Don't discount the value of thanking people for their time, since time is money!

1. Set up a timeline for thanking those who give you their time.

2. If someone has given you her time in the last month and you haven't thanked her, commit to do it within the next week.

Method #5

Anniversary of Business

This is a really great touch. When you're tracking a client's anniversary of doing business with you, it shows you're really paying attention to the relationship. If you operate a transactional business, you can still track anniversaries. This is most impressive, because you're not seeing that client on a regular basis through repeat business.

If a transactional business does get repeat business, there's usually a time gap between transactions, i.e., realtors, mortgage brokers, home improvement contractors, architects, etc. If you've never tracked anniversaries and it's been five years since you transacted business with a client, that's OK. When you reach out to him just say you can't believe it's been five years. This way, you're focusing on the five-year anniversary, which will deflect from the fact that you haven't stayed in touch for five years.

Create traditions around the anniversary. If you work for an employer, take the client to lunch with the president/owner, sales manager or anyone else who plays a significant role in your company. You might bring in lunch for your client's staff, or your tradition might be something as small as a phone call to say happy anniversary or meeting for a drink at a local coffee house.

Case in Point

I signed up a new client who owns a car dealership. My next step was to schedule a time for program training. I asked him when would be a good time to get together, and he told me the following week would work. He suggested I bring in lunch for him and a few of his staff members. I thought it was a little early in the relationship to bring in lunch, but I certainly wasn't going to say no. He told me they like a Chinese takeout restaurant down the street and suggested I call the office the morning of our meeting to get everyone's order.

I immediately made note of the restaurant and knew that would be our anniversary tradition. I brought lunch in the following week and ate with him and his staff. I enjoyed getting to know his team and through the normal course of conversation, they asked what I did. We talked about my card program and my background. After lunch, I did some training with my client. Before I left the premises, I was approached by one of the men from lunch, who told me he wanted to sign up for my program. We arranged a time for me to follow up with him and I drove away with a new prospect. You never know what will come out of creating traditions and staying in touch.

 ## "Get The Ball Rolling" Action Steps

The more you can personalize your relationships with clients, the better your chances are at keeping them long term. Creating an anniversary date tradition might be right up your alley.

1. Print out your client list and determine anniversary dates. This may take some research if you haven't tracked this before.

2. Enter the anniversary dates into your reminder system.

3. Determine what traditions you'll create, based on your knowledge of your client.

Method #6

Birthdays

This is one of the easiest ways to reach out. If you're in a business that requires you to get clients' birthday information for business reasons, such as banking, life insurance or financial planning, take advantage of having that information at your fingertips. If your business doesn't require getting birthday information, decide at what point you're going to ask clients for their birthdays. If you don't do it at the same time during your prospecting/sales process, it becomes haphazard and inconsistent.

Get birthdays for your prospects, referral sources and anyone else who's important to you and your business. Of course, you'll want to send a birthday card...the "old-fashioned" way, through the mail. Ecards just don't have the same impact a physical card does and it takes next to no effort to wish someone happy birthday through a social media site. You may also want to send a gift or take the person to lunch or dinner, depending on the relationship.

When you send a birthday card, don't include your business card. The birthday touch is about them and not about you and your business. With the Follow Up Savvy System, not only do you send a card and/or gift, but you'll also call them on their birthday. This is very powerful. A birthday call really makes the person you're calling feel special and it leaves an outstanding impression. When you make the birthday call, don't bring up business; the call is not about you.

Having said that, what ends up happening many times is through the natural course of conversation, the birthday boy will want to know how you and your business are doing. You can then engage in conversation about your business if *he* brings it up. You may find he wants to give you a referral or do some business with you. I recently received three referrals from my birthday calls. I'm convinced this happens because when you show people you care about them and remember them, they're interested in helping you. I don't ever ask for referrals or bring up business on birthday calls, but it's amazing how many times I hang up with more business and/or referrals.

I've had many people ask me how to ask for someone's birthday. I merely say I'm putting your contact information into my database and would like to include your birthday. Most of the time, I get a favorable response. If someone tells me she doesn't celebrate birthdays, I ask if she celebrates holidays. The reason for that follow-up question is because some people may not celebrate these occasions for religious reasons. If this is the case, I simply make note of it and reach out in other ways. Once in a while, people will say they don't celebrate birthdays because they just don't like them. I make note of this as well and reach out at holidays and other times.

Action Step #1 below suggests putting the birthdays of your **existing** clients, prospects, referral sources and others important to the success of your business into your database program. If you don't have this information, you'll need to contact them and ask for it. This is OK, because it's a great reason to touch them and reconnect if it's been awhile.

Case in Point

One of my clients, Norma, is a mortgage broker. She's been in the mortgage business for 30 years and has been sending birthday cards for 20 years. She sends on average 150 birthday cards a month. She told me that she gets seven to eight loans a month from those cards. Since sending a birthday card isn't truly marketing, I'd say those seven to eight loans are generating a healthy return on investment.

"Get The Ball Rolling" Action Steps

Most people love being remembered on their birthday, so this is an easy way to score some big "touch points."

1. Input birthdays into your database program for your existing clients, prospects, referral sources and anyone else who's important to your business.

2. Figure out how and at what point in your prospecting/selling process you're going to ask for birthdays.

3. Decide how you'll reach out for birthdays.

4. Schedule a time of day when you'll make your birthday calls and stick to it.

Method #7

Holidays are a really great way to reach out. With the Follow Up Savvy System, you'll think outside the December holiday "box." The problem with sending holiday cards in December is that so many people send cards at the same time. If you do send out cards in December, get them out no later than the first week of the month. If they go out later than that, they'll get caught with the masses. For all you know, a receptionist or administrative assistant is opening your card and taping it to the wall without the intended recipient ever seeing it or knowing you've reached out.

If your card goes out early in the month, you'll stand out. You'll be thought of as being organized and ahead of schedule, which will leave a great impression. You may also choose to stand out by sending cards for Thanksgiving or New Year's instead of the traditional December holiday greetings. Not many send cards for these occasions.

There are many other holidays throughout the year. If you Google holidays in any given year, most months have between two and four of them. Think about reaching out on Valentine's Day, St. Patrick's Day, Cinco de Mayo, Independence Day, Halloween, etc. There are many ways to be different during holiday times; you can even choose to "commemorate" Daylight Savings Time.

Case in Point #1

Norma, my mortgage broker client, sends cards to everyone in her database four times a year and she never sends them in December. She believes sending December cards is a wasted effort for the reasons I've discussed above. I've already told you she sends an average of 150 birthday cards a month. I talked to her assistant recently and she told me they were sending out 3,000 cards for the 4th of July, which may sound outrageous.

I recently saw Norma and learned she had $40 million in her pipeline ready to close by the end of the month. Her biggest stress point was she didn't have enough staff to get everything closed. It seems to me that a $40 million pipeline is more outrageous than sending 3,000 cards.

The real estate market is struggling and most mortgage brokers I've talked to recently are hanging on by a thread, barely getting by, telling me how slow it is and how hard deals are to come by. I find it no coincidence that Norma's business is thriving based on the effort she puts forth to stay in touch.

Case in Point #2

I showed a demo of my card program to a prospect who owns a tile company. She loved the program and said it was exactly what they're looking for. She asked me to follow up with her the first of the following month, which was October, to get signed up. I called her at that time and got no response. I called and emailed her the second week and got no response. When it came to time contact her the third week, I wondered if I should just call and email again. I came to the conclusion that I wanted to do something different to get her attention and a response. Halloween was around the corner. I wasn't sure what her thoughts were about October 31, but I decided to send her a Halloween card with a few caramels. She called me the day she received them and said she was ready to get signed up. I was in her office two days later, completing the transaction and training her staff. This illustrates how you can even use holidays for your prospecting efforts.

"Get The Ball Rolling" Action Steps

Holidays present a great opportunity to reach out, and if you're limiting yourself to the traditional December holiday period, you're missing out on the chance to separate yourself from the pack.

1. Research all the holidays that occur throughout the year.

2. Choose the holidays on which you'll reach out and commit to doing so consistently, year in and year out.

Method #8

HOW AM I DOING?
IS THERE ANYTHING I CAN DO FOR YOU?

This is a very powerful way to reach out over the phone. This call is to simply check in and see how your clients are doing with your services or product and if they have any other needs. Even if you're in a transactional business, this touch can work. You can call one month, six months, one year or two years later to get feedback on your clients' experiences with your product or service. You never know what will come out of these calls, but they will leave a great impression because they show you care and haven't forgotten about them.

Don't be surprised if you hear the person you're calling say he was just thinking of you or has been meaning to call. It's crazy how this works, but it does. It's such a great feeling when you hear those words. If you do this consistently, you *will* hear them.

Case in Point

My client, Kirk Henson, owns Henson & Son/Fix Auto in Escondido, California. His shop did some repair work on my car. Several days after my car was fixed, I received a phone call from a representative at his shop wanting to know how my experience was, how my car was doing and if there was anything else I needed. When I hung up, I thought, "wow," that was really nice. It left a great impression.

"Get The Ball Rolling" Action Steps

Checking up with clients is a powerful way to gain loyalty and make them feel good about doing business with you.

1. Create a checking-in call list made up of current and past clients.

2. Decide how often you want to check in.

3. Commit to making a minimum of three calls a week until you're caught up.

Method #9

This is a great touch that you'll want to do only by phone. You're calling clients just because you're thinking of them and want to know how they're doing. This is different than the checking-in call because there's no agenda other than the recipient of the call. It's not about business; this is the call where clients may open up to you on a personal level.

When that happens, you're in the process of deepening that relationship. Your client may tell you he got promoted, he's taking a great European trip, he's having surgery, he's going to be a parent/grandparent, he likes baseball and the local team, or a host of other events going on in his life. In addition to providing you with great personal insight, making this call also gives you the opportunity to follow up again.

Let's say your client is going on a great vacation; you can make note of that and call him when he returns to see how it was. If he's going to have surgery, you can send him a get well card and follow up with a phone call to see how he's doing. If you found out he likes baseball and the local team, you can make note of that and invite him to join you or give him tickets to an upcoming game.

This call gives you a great opportunity to show clients you care about them beyond business. When your intention is strictly business, that's the type of conversation you'll have. When your intention doesn't involve business, you have an opportunity to take the relationship to a whole new level. Make one *Just Because* call a day. Many times, you'll get a voicemail and the call will take 10 seconds. If you're lucky, your client will pick up and you'll have an opportunity to reconnect.

When giving my Follow Up Savvy presentations, I've been asked on more than one occasion what to say on a *Just Because* call. Every time I'm asked this question, it makes me realize how out of touch people are with those in their life. If I get a voicemail, I say, "Hi Jan, this is Wanda. I was thinking of you and wanted to check in and see how you're doing. Give me a call when you get a minute. Nothing urgent; just calling to say hi. Take care and have a great day." Jan may or may not call me back, and even if she doesn't, at least she knows I was thinking of her.

When my call is answered, I say, "Hi Jill, this is Wanda. I was thinking of you and wanted to check in and see how you're doing." The conversation will take off from there. One of the fun results of this call is when do you get the person on the phone and she realizes you really don't want anything, she hangs up thinking, "wow, she *did* just call to say hi."

Have you ever received a call from someone who claims they're calling to say hi and when you hang up you realize they really wanted something? It doesn't leave you with a good feeling. If you're calling for something, say so; don't try to trick people by saying you're calling to say hi. With the *Just Because* call, you truly are calling just to say hi and there's no hidden agenda.

Case in Point

I gave one of my Follow Up Savvy presentations to a sales team at a printing company. The week following my presentation, one of the salesmen, Ron, made a *Just Because* call to a woman who oversees print production for another company. Because her company has its own printing department, it's never needed Ron's services. Ron always liked this woman and decided she'd be his *Just Because* call for this particular day. She was happy to hear from him and told him she'd been thinking about him. She said her company was very busy and was thinking about outsourcing some print work.

Ron had no intention of possibly getting business from this call, because he knew the company did its own print work. He was genuinely calling to see how she was doing. He didn't care that there wasn't business there for him (or so he thought); he just wanted to say hi. When he hung up, he had some potential new business. You never know what will come from simply showing someone you care and are thinking of them. Don't second-guess or rule out making a *Just Because* call to a competitor. Make the call to say hi if you truly like and care for the person.

 ## "Get The Ball Rolling" Action Steps

"Just because" calls can result in unexpected bonuses...since you have no agenda at all other than saying hi when you make them.

1. Note the clients, vendors, prospects, competitors, etc. to whom you want to make *Just Because* calls.

2. Schedule one *Just Because* call a day. Put it on your calendar as if it's an appointment.

Principle 5

How Effective Follow Up
Turns into First-Class Service

When I was a banker, I went through extensive customer service training. What I came to realize is follow up is a form and an extension of customer service. For some, the idea of follow up is burdensome because it's one more thing that needs to be done. If you feel this way, you should shift your thinking and focus on the fact that follow up is nothing more than giving great customer service.

If you've had a great customer service experience, I'm sure you'd agree it made you feel good, you remembered the experience, you want to continue to do business with the person who treated you so well, and you're open to referring that person/business. When you follow up and stay in touch, you're giving exceptional service. Your clients will remember you, they'll feel good about you, they'll want to continue to do business with you and they'll tell others about you.

Traits of first-class service include:

- You return phone calls and emails in a timely manner.

- You're **ALWAYS** friendly.

- You don't appear rushed or hurried.

- You make your clients, prospects and referral sources feel important.

- You show appreciation.

If you display these traits, you'll be seen as being attentive and respectful of your relationships. If you don't exhibit them, you run the risk of becoming neglectful of your relationships. Don't run around in a frenzied state of mind and forget about the importance of serving the people who are the lifeblood of your business in a first-class way. View your clients, prospects and referral sources as VIPs. Have a "roll out the red carpet" mentality *every* time you deal with them. Let them know you're excited about working with them and you appreciate them. Be conscious of your energy level.

Let's take a look at the traits that make up first-class service.

Trait #1 – You Return Phone Calls And Emails In A Timely Manner

There are some time management philosophies that advocate returning phone calls and checking emails during certain times of day. I'm going to give you another perspective on this. I certainly understand you can't drop whatever you're doing every time your phone rings or an email comes in. However, you can manage communication effectively by responding to the email or phone call at your earliest convenience, remaining responsive to the person contacting you. Take on the mindset that business is more about your clients/prospects/referral sources than it is about you. I'm not saying to let them manage you, but you do need to create a time management system that takes first-class service into consideration.

I've heard voicemails that say, "I return phone calls between 10:00 and 11:00 and 4:00 and 5:00." It may or may not be OK if I learn that my call at 10:15 won't be returned until after 4:00. I love it when my competitors are on this system, because I know I'll give better service.

Even if you can't return a call until 4:00, is it really necessary to say that? Also, if you use this type of recording and you return a call at 2:00, you're not doing what your voicemail says...so the system could appear to be a mechanism to screen calls. Think about returning phone calls when you get to a good stopping point.

Make a point to return all phone calls, even those from salespeople selling things that aren't of interest to you. You don't want to be viewed as someone who doesn't return phone calls. Everyone is worthy of a returned phone call; it goes back to impressions. If you leave a good impression, you never know what will come from it.

While salespeople who call you may not be able to help you with your business or be potential clients, you never know who they know. If they're impressed with your response and you treat them respectfully, there may come a day when they can help you in some way. Treat everyone with respect.

I know people who don't return emails for 24-48 hours. Again, I love it if my competitors have this practice in place, because I know I'll be much faster to respond. I was surprised to hear a recent luncheon speaker tell our group that she returns emails within 48 hours. I wonder how she can stand out and be exceptional in her prospects' and clients' eyes with that kind of timeline. I think you open the door to potential frustration if someone's sent you an email and doesn't get a response for 48 hours. That's two days, and a lot can happen in that time. This timeline may work for some people, including that speaker, but how does it work for their clients and prospects?

Be cognizant of the emails you send. Everyone's in-boxes are inundated. Before hitting "send," ask yourself:

- Am I sending this email because it's convenient for me?

- Would it be easier for the recipient if I *talked* to him about this matter?

- Could this be resolved quicker with verbal communication?

- Is this a cumbersome email that will result in a deferred response?

Remembering first-class service may prevent you from sending unnecessary emails.

One last thing I want to say about emails is respond to **all** of them, no matter how small the response may be. This lets the sender know you received it. Even if the response is two words, respond. Don't leave the sender wondering if you got his email.

You may be thinking, what's the big deal? I got the email; that's what's important. It goes beyond that. It's about being attentive. It may seem like a minor detail, but it's an important one. If you take shortcuts for minor details, it may appear that you'll take them for major details as well.

I love the saying, "how you do anything is how you do everything." This keeps me on track and doesn't allow me to get lazy. Not responding to an email is as big a violation as not returning a phone call. Remember, we're talking about first-class service. When you're operating in first-class fashion, there's no room for neglect or shortcuts.

When you establish a reputation for always returning phone calls and emails in a timely manner, this naturally builds confidence with your clients, prospects and referral sources. Once this reputation is established, if you have a day where you just couldn't get back to someone, that person will know you must be busy because you always get back to her. There's no panic or frustration. Being responsive is a powerful way to build your reputation.

Don't lose sight of first-class service when establishing your timelines and system.

Trait #2 – You're *Always* Friendly

This doesn't mean you're happy and friendly 24/7. What it means is you're always friendly when communicating with your clients, prospects and referral sources. Regardless of what's going on, they deserve to be treated in a friendly manner. When you're always friendly, your clients won't have to deal with inconsistent moods. If you're outwardly moody, your clients won't know what they're going to get when they deal with you. Be stable.

The saying, "kill 'em with kindness" is powerful. It's very hard to be mad, frustrated or upset with someone who's kind and friendly.

If you have the reputation for always being friendly, you'll be granted much more forgiveness in any given situation than someone who's not known for being friendly. If you or your company make an error, it will be much easier for your clients to forgive the situation because you're friendly.

I'm sure you've had a customer service experience when the person you're dealing with was unfriendly. It's not a pleasant experience. Don't be that person or give that experience to your clients. They deserve first-class service.

If you're a business owner and have a receptionist, it's very important to make sure that person represents you well and is friendly from the word hello. You can absolutely hear a smile over the phone. Receptionists are the first impression of a business. I called a business recently and after I asked for the person I wanted to contact, the receptionist didn't say anything; I just got a click in my ear. My first thought was, "how rude." Then I thought: "Was she rushed?" "Is she having a bad day or does she just not like her job?" "Does the owner know how unfriendly she is?" These aren't questions anyone should have to ask themselves when they're calling a business. That receptionist may be the nicest person in the world, but her customer service skills weren't showing that…and it soured the impression of the business.

Trait #3 – You Don't Appear Rushed or Hurried

If you're in a hurry, you'll compromise your level of service. Have you ever barely been given the time to tell a waitress your order at a restaurant? It's very uncomfortable and is an example of poor service. What about when you call someone and it's obvious the person is in a hurry and is trying to end the conversation prematurely. This also compromises service. If you don't have time or it's not a good time, don't pick up the phone, return the email or do anything else that will result in less than first-class service. Wait until you can give your undivided attention.

Trait #4 – You Make Your Clients, Prospects and Referral Sources Feel Important

If you implement the Follow Up Savvy principles, this will happen automatically. Stay in touch, be friendly and let your clients, prospects and referral sources know how much you care. When you're dealing with them, your goal should be to make them feel like the most important person in the world.

Trait #5 – You Show Appreciation

This book contains numerous ways to show appreciation. Implement them and your clients, prospects and referral sources will never doubt your appreciation for them.

It can be of great value to collect personal information on your clients, prospects and referral sources, such as their favorite restaurant for lunch and dinner, their favorite wine, if they drink coffee, their hobbies, if they like sporting events, and whatever else you'd like to know about them. You can gather this information by simply asking for it or you can listen closely during your conversations to see if they reveal some of their personal "likes." Keep this information in the notes section of your database. It comes in handy when you want to appreciate them in a unique way; your personalization efforts will make them feel very special.

Nordstrom and Southwest Airlines are two companies that include customer service as a big part of their branding. When you walk into any Nordstrom, you know you're going to be treated well. They've worked hard to build a "customer-first" reputation. When I fly on Southwest, I know I'm going to laugh and be entertained, since the airline has built its reputation on having fun. What reputation have you built for yourself?

Case in Point

I mentioned earlier that Henson & Son/Fix Auto did some repair work on my car. Gina, their receptionist, is truly the friendliest person I've seen at a front desk. She's happy when she answers the phone, she gets excited when she hears who's calling and she's willing to address any request. She creates a great first impression for Henson & Son and continuously makes great impressions.

During my car's repair process, I received several emails from Gina. In one of them, the salutation was Hi Wanda! Notice the exclamation point after my name. I could feel her excitement even over an email. Another email had a smiley face on it. She exudes friendliness in person, over the phone and electronically. I can't tell you if she's friendly 24/7, but I can tell you, every time I've dealt with Gina she's been extremely friendly.

When my car was ready, I picked it up and on the way home I noticed a rattle in the back end. I called the shop and Gina answered. I told her about the rattle, she made me feel like there would be no problem at all, and she forwarded me to the estimator who worked on my car. He was also very friendly and told me to bring my car in the next morning. While my car was being worked on, I sat in the reception area and observed Gina for 30 minutes. She never lost her enthusiasm and excitement with the customers who were calling or coming into the shop. She's such a breath of fresh air; I truly enjoyed watching and listening to her.

If your car has been hit and you're in need of auto repair work, it can be a very stressful time. When dealing with a company that has a "Gina" manning the front desk, your stress level immediately goes down. I'd be so happy to refer Henson & Son/Fix Auto to anyone in need of auto repair work. I know everyone I refer will get first-class service starting with Gina and continuing with all other team members. They've figured out what first- class service is and does. It's no wonder they've been in business for 27 years.

I called Kirk Henson, the owner of Henson & Son, to get his permission to use his company in this book. I also told him I was going to discuss Gina. He told me she used to work at a deli he frequented for lunch; she was always very friendly and remembered what each customer ordered for lunch. He saw these outstanding customer service traits and approached her about working for him. The rest is history.

You never know what opportunities will come your way from the simple act of being friendly.

"Get The Ball Rolling" Action Steps

What are you doing to ensure you provide first-class service to clients, prospects and referral sources?

1. Ask yourself, "What reputation have I built for myself?" Write down what you can do to improve it.

2. Ask yourself, "If I were my client, prospect or referral source, would I be happy with the service I'm providing?" Write down areas where you can improve.

3. Establish a timeline for returning phone calls and emails.

4. Commit to acknowledging all emails even if the response is only two words.

5. If you have employees, make sure they're giving first-class service on your behalf. Enroll them in customer service classes, hire shoppers who'll rate your customer service or implement an employee reward/recognition program focused on great customer service.

PRINCIPLE 6

OUTSHINE YOUR COMPETITION

According to a study by Dartnell and McGraw Hill:

- 48% of salespeople never follow up

- 80% of sales are made after the fifth contact

- 10% of salespeople make more than three contacts

These statistics are astounding. They should immediately and forever change the way you view your competition, once you implement the Follow Up Savvy System. If you're networking and you and one of your competitors meet the same great prospect, you'll know there's a 48% chance your competitor won't follow up. At the same time, you'll be confident in your follow-up efforts because you have a system that includes specific timelines. You'll respond within 48 hours of meeting a new prospect, and you adhere to a system that supports making as many contacts as necessary to close the business.

Being in the top 10 percentile is a given with the Follow Up Savvy System. Remember, as discussed in Principle 1, you'll create prospects' loyalty before they've said yes and even after they've said no. You're primed, both mentally and systematically, for making more than three contacts.

Most prospects don't buy on the spot. They'll tell you they need to think about it and will get back to you. When you hear those words, it's critical to have a follow-up conversation. You should always end your prospecting meetings by asking if it's OK for you to follow up; most times, people will say yes, and if they say they'll get back to you, be sure to ask if you can contact them if that doesn't happen. In both cases, ask what time would be good for them to hear from you.

By asking these questions, you're in control of the next follow-up step. When you get back to a prospect, you can say, "when we last spoke, you said this would be a good time to follow up with you." This will take away any awkwardness or discomfort about following up. You're reminding them *they* said this was a good time for them. You may ask these questions numerous times during a sales cycle until you land the business.

When I was a banker, I can't tell you how many times I had prospects tell me they never heard from their banker. This always surprised me, because I couldn't imagine having a client and not ever touching them after business was transacted. Because I heard this so frequently, I knew it wouldn't take much effort on my part to outshine my competition. It was almost embarrassing that the bar was so low.

I knew if I could convert prospects to clients, they'd be pleasantly surprised, based on what they were used to, by my follow-up and staying-in-touch habits. The Follow Up Savvy System raises the bar significantly. Once your clients, prospects and referral sources get accustomed to the kind of service you provide, you'll receive a tremendous amount of appreciation and loyalty.

Your goal should be to never stop following up and staying in touch. By doing so, you'll absolutely outshine your competition and will always leave clients, prospects and referral sources with a positive impression. As a bonus, they'll never forget about you. Consistently reaching out will absolutely give you a competitive advantage.

Case in Point

I met my client, Ted, at a Chamber of Commerce networking event. The sales cycle with him was 10 months. During that time, I made five phone calls and sent six cards. The cards I sent were nice to meet you, thank you for the referral, information on my card program, Happy Holidays, April Fools and a confirmation card for our demo appointment. In the 10th month, he agreed to see a demo of my program. I made 11 contacts before I was able to set up the demo appointment on August 3. After seeing the demo, he told me he liked the program and said he was interested in signing up, but he wanted to wait until the following month, after he'd paid his kids' college tuition.

The annual convention for SendOutCards was scheduled for August 17 and the owner, Kody Bateman, threw out a challenge to distributors that I was one person away from meeting. I made numerous calls trying to get one of my prospects to sign up before August 17. I was getting down to the wire and told myself I needed to call Ted. On August 11, I decided to call and see if he'd be open to bumping up his decision by a few weeks. I was nervous about making this call, but I knew I had to do it.

One good thing about challenges is they take you out of your comfort zone. Making this call was definitely going to do that for me. I called Ted and said, "This is a bold call. You expressed an interest in signing up for the program in September, but I'm wondering if there's any chance you'd be open to doing it by tomorrow?" I told him I was trying to meet a challenge and was one person away from doing so. There was definite hesitation in his voice, and he asked me to call him the next morning.

I made that call and got his voicemail. By 2:30, I still hadn't heard from him, so I called again. This time he answered. He apologized for not getting back to me and asked if I'd found one more person to sign up. I told him no. He said he really did want to wait until September and I thought, "oh no, he's not going to sign up early." To my surprise, he continued: "you're very professional and have been great at following up with me. I'm a sucker for that so I'll go ahead and sign up." I was over the moon. He helped me meet the challenge, and reinforced my philosophy about how being good at follow up can benefit you in so many great ways.

Don't give up, don't get discouraged and be determined to outshine your competition. Implementing the Follow Up Savvy System and completing the "Get the Ball Rolling" Action Steps will put you in the elite 10% and keep you there.

"Get the Ball Rolling" Action Steps

When you communicate regularly with your clients, prospects and referral sources, and you're prepared for the follow-up process, you'll be outperforming 90% of your competitors.

1. Create scenarios that may happen as you communicate with your target audience, e.g., it's not a good time for me to buy, I'm not authorized to make a decision, etc.

2. Role-play ways to respond to these scenarios, starting with asking permission to follow up and then making that next call.

PRINCIPLE 7

3 MUSTS FOR AN EFFECTIVE FOLLOW-UP SYSTEM

It's critical to have your follow-up efforts systematized. As mentioned numerous times throughout this book, without a good system in place, your actions will be haphazard and become inconsistent, which results in being ineffective. Three musts are outlined below that will help you keep the Follow Up Savvy System in place.

Must #1 – Timelines

Timelines will keep you on track and create boundaries for you. Set them and commit to them. No matter how much planning and forethought you put toward a follow-up system, not sticking to your timelines will undermine your efforts.

Must #2 – Reminder System

This is critical to your success. If you're collecting birthdays, but don't have a system that reminds you of them, how can you effectively get cards, gifts or birthday calls done? If a prospect or client tells you to call back next week, next month or next year, you need a reminder system to alert you when it's time to do it. The reminder system needs to be automated.

Must #3 – Choose a Time of Day

It's important to choose a specific time of day to get all your follow-up work completed. I've tried different times throughout the day and what works best for me is the morning. I make my birthday calls, follow-up calls and get any cards, emails or other correspondence out that pertain to follow up before noon. If follow up isn't a part of your everyday schedule, it will fall by the wayside. You have to make it a part of your day, just like checking emails, voicemails and social media sites. It should have a top priority.

Once your timelines, reminder system and time of day are in place, you're on your way to experiencing a new level of success in your business.

Case in Point

I make my follow-up calls at 9:00 every morning. If I have a morning meeting that delays me, I get very uncomfortable until I get those calls done. On a rare occasion, I won't be able to make them until the afternoon and I'm really squirming by then. It's such a habit for me that I'm extremely uncomfortable when I can't stick to my timeline.

"Get The Ball Rolling" Action Steps

Be sure you do everything you can to ensure the success of your follow-up system over the long term.

1. As suggested in each principle, create timelines for all the ways you've committed to following up.

2. Get reminder dates set up in your database program.

3. Decide on the time of day you'll handle your follow-up responsibilities and stick to it.

CONCLUSION

The Follow Up Savvy System has been tried and tested. I've achieved some great successes and it's given me an extreme amount of confidence. Anything that will boost your confidence in the sales and business-building world is a huge benefit. Why not create some confidence by implementing these principles and giving yourself a competitive edge?

I recently put this system to the ultimate test. Our CEO made some adjustments to the four SendOutCards packages, and in rolling them out, gave all distributors a challenge. We were asked to bring in five new clients in one week; one had to sign up for the top package but the other four could sign up for any of the other packages. I completed the challenge in week 1.

The same challenge was put out for two additional weeks, and I met it two more times. The overall goal was to sign up 15 new clients in three weeks. I exceeded that and signed up 18 new clients. I'd never experienced that level of production before. It was intense. I'd stretched myself in ways I never would have done on my own.

When the challenge was over, the distributors who hit the challenge all three weeks were posted on the SendOutCards website. Out of more than 100,000 distributors, only 15 did it and I was one of them. I'm not telling you this to impress you or brag about myself; I want to drive home the point that if you have an effective follow-up and staying-in-touch system, you can achieve a goal such as this one.

I wouldn't have reached this goal if I didn't have the Follow Up Savvy System in place. I can't speak for the other 14 people who hit the mark all three weeks, but I can tell you how I did it. I knew I didn't have time to go out and find new prospects for this challenge. I had to rely on the people I already knew and those who'd already seen the program. These were prospects who didn't sign up for one reason or another. In other words, they were people who'd told me no.

Because I had established a system that supported me in consistently staying in touch with them, even after they said no, I was very comfortable picking up the phone and telling them about the new packages. I called several prospects who'd seen demos two years earlier. I didn't experience a moment of discomfort, awkwardness or embarrassment when asking them to reconsider the program with the new packages and pricing. This was invaluable for me. This experience validated everything I've practiced since creating the Follow Up Savvy System.

As you begin putting the Follow Up Savvy System in place, you may question yourself and the principles. That's your ego fighting against change. Many times, when we're thinking and operating from an ego standpoint, we can enter an irrational state of mind. You can talk yourself into or out of anything. Be very careful not to talk yourself out of implementing this system because it's uncomfortable or awkward. These principles are nothing more than habits. As with any new behavior you want to turn into a habit, it's uncomfortable when you start. Once the habit is formed, however, it will be uncomfortable *not* to do it. Before you know it, these principles will become second nature.

Another irrational thought you may have and must be careful of is, "I don't have the time for this." I cringe when I hear someone say that. We're all given the same amount of time. How you choose to use it is entirely up to you. We all have different life circumstances, but if you're in a business-building or sales production career, making time for follow up is imperative. The busier your life is, the more critical it is to follow these principles. They'll help keep your business life streamlined—more efficient and productive.

Be careful not to fall into the thought trap of, "I don't have enough prospects/clients to implement a follow-up system." Those words also make me cringe. My immediate thought is that you don't think the few contacts you have are worthy of hearing from you. If you're just starting out, this is the *perfect* time to implement a system. Why wait until you have hundreds of contacts? It will be far more time-consuming and take much more energy to form the habits and implement the system when you're dealing with hundreds rather than a few. Without a system, you run the risk of being neglectful of your relationships whether they're a few, hundreds or thousands.

I've been faithfully following up with a prospect for two years. She was referred to me by a business associate. She hasn't been interested in my program, but I believe it just hasn't been the right time. Since our initial contact, I've called her eight times and sent her 10 cards. I talked to her recently and she commented on how much my consistent follow up impresses her. She's mentioned this to me before, but on this particular call, she also said "Wanda, if you ever want to get into the real estate business, I'd love to have you on my team."

Keep in mind, I've never met her before and she knows nothing about my background, but in spite of that, she'd still like to work with me based solely on my follow-up habits. I've had other job offers because of the impression my follow-up efforts has made.

Great follow up definitely leaves an impression that can bring great, unexpected opportunities your way. If you button down this system, you'll experience successes and opportunities that you weren't counting on.

I hope this book has motivated and inspired you to take your relationships and business to a new level. Commit to becoming a master at follow up. Do yourself a favor and "Get the Ball Rolling"!

May you always dream big, live well and enjoy the ride.

About the Author

Wanda Allen does speaking engagements for corporate sales teams, entrepreneurs and business organizations. She also presents workshops and does consulting work based on the Follow Up Savvy Principles. If you're interested in contacting her to schedule one of these events or you'd like additional copies of Follow Up Savvy, go to FollowUpSavvy.com

Notes:

Notes:

Made in the USA
Charleston, SC
15 June 2014